SCIFA

May 2024

MW01526891

*

THE STAFF OF SCIFAIKUEST:
TERI SANTITORO, EDITOR

SCIFAIKUEST is published quarterly online and in print. The two editions are different.

Cover art by Richard Schell
Cover design by Laura Givens

Vol. XXI, No. 4   May 2024
Scifaikuest [ISSN 1558-9730] is published quarterly on the 1st day of February, May, August, and November in the United States of America by Hiraeth Publishing, P.O. Box 1248, Tularosa, NM 88352. Copyright 2024 by Hiraeth Publishing. All rights revert to authors and artists upon publication.
Writers and artists guidelines are available online at https://www.hiraethsffh.com/scifaikuest.
Guidelines are also available upon request from Hiraeth Publishing, P.O. Box 1248, Tularosa, NM, 88352, if request is accompanied by a SASE #10 envelope with a first-class US stamp. Subscriptions: $28 for one year [4 issues], $44 for two years [8 issues]. Single copies $9.00 postage paid in the United States. Subscriptions to Canada: $33 for one year, $51 for two years. Single copies $11.00 postage paid to Canada. U.S. and Canadian subscribers remit in U.S. funds. All other countries inquire about rates.

What???
No subscription to
Scifaikuest??

We can fix that . . .

https://www.hiraethsffh.com/product -page/scifaikuest-1

Or get a sample back issue to check us out!

https://www.hiraethsffh.com /shop-1

And a subscription makes a great gift, for a holiday or any time of the year!

Minimalism:
A Handbook of Minimalist Genre Poetic Forms

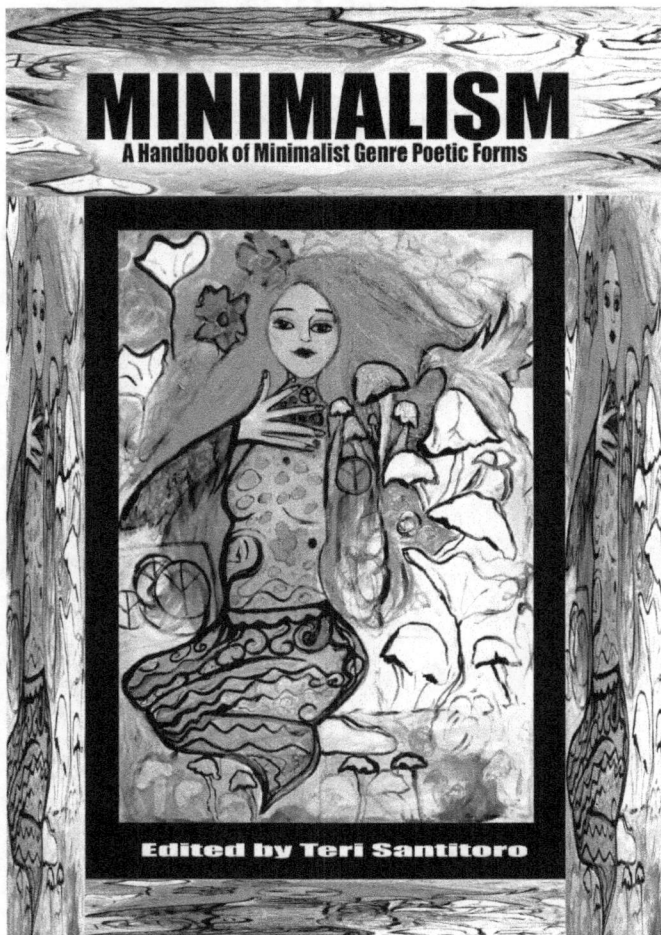

MINIMALISM
A Handbook of Minimalist Genre Poetic Forms

Edited by Teri Santitoro

This handbook contains articles about how to write various minimalist poetry forms such as scifaiku, senryu, sijo, haibun, empat perkataan, ghazals, cinquain, cherita, rengays, rengu, octains, tanka, threesomes, and many more. Each article is written by an expert in that particular poetry form.

Teri Santitoro, aka sakyu, who assembled this handbook, has been the editor of Scifaikuest since 2003.

https://www.hiraethsffh.com/product-page/minimalism-a-handbook-of-minimalist-genre-poetic-forms

A Little Help, Please

In the world of the small indie press we fight a never-ending battle for attention to our work, as writers and in publishing. Here's an example: big publishers [you know who they are] have gobs of $$$ that they can devote to advertising and marketing. Here at Hiraeth Publishing, our advertising budget consists of the deposits for whatever soda bottles and aluminum cans we can find alongside the highways. Anti-littering laws make our task even more difficult . . . ☺

That's where YOU come in. YOU are our best promoter. YOU are the one who can tell others about us. Just send 'em to our website, tell them about our store. That's all. Just that.

Of course, we don't mind if you talk us up. We're pretty good, you know. We have some award-winning and award-nominated writers and artists, plus other voices well-deserving to be heard [not everyone wins awards, right?] but our publications are read-worthy nevertheless.

That number once again is:

www.hiraethsffh.com

Friend us on Facebook at Hiraeth Publishing

Follow us on Twitter at @HiraethPublish1

SALE!!

There's a sale going on!! It's still going on!!

All the books you can order at 20% off the total! Woot!

Buy 1 book; buy 100 books! It's all the same discount. Use the code **BOOKS2024** when you check out.

Go to the Shop at www.hiraethsffh.com and make those selections now!

You'll be glad you did. So will we.

EDITORIAL

Greetings, and Happy May Day!
I hope your Spring has finally sprung! As we leave winter behind, let's try to remember to be as kind as the soft breezes of the season!

Our Cover art is *Three Body Problem* by the ever-talented **Richard E. Schell**, and our Featured Poet is that dynamic wordsmith, **Lisa Timpf!**

Don't miss my favorite poem by **Randall Andrews**!

Scifaikuest now has its own ISBN!!! Please inform your local book stores and library that they are now able to ORDER SCIFAIKUEST!!!

You can now find us at Hiraeth Books at:
https://www.hiraethsffh.com/home-1

If you don't have a subscription to our PRINT edition, they are available at:
https://www.hiraethsffh.com/product-page/scifaikuest

And, if you would like to join the select group of contributors by submitting your poetry, artwork or article, you can find our guidelines at:
https://www.hiraethsffh.com/scifaikuest

You can also read our ONLINE VERSION at:
https://www.hiraethsffh.com/scifaikuest-online

Pssst! Looking for something good to read?

You can get t.santitoro's newest novella, Those Who Die, at:
THOSE WHO DIE by t. santitoro | Hiraeth Publishing (hiraethsffh.com)
You can also order **t.santitoro's** latest novella, *Adopted Child,* at:

https://www.hiraethsffh.com/product-page/adopted-child-by-t-santitoro

You can also get a copy of her novelette, *The Legend of Trey Valentine,* at:
https://www.hiraethsffh.com/product-page/legend-of-trey-valentine-by-teri-santitoro

A huge Scifaikuest Welcome and let's hear it for our newest contributors: **Randy Brooks, Ruben Horn, Matthew Johnston, Goran Lowie, Juan M. Perez**

Martian May Day
remembering the flowers
on Earth

-sakyu-

Aliens, Magic, and Monsters
By Lauren McBride

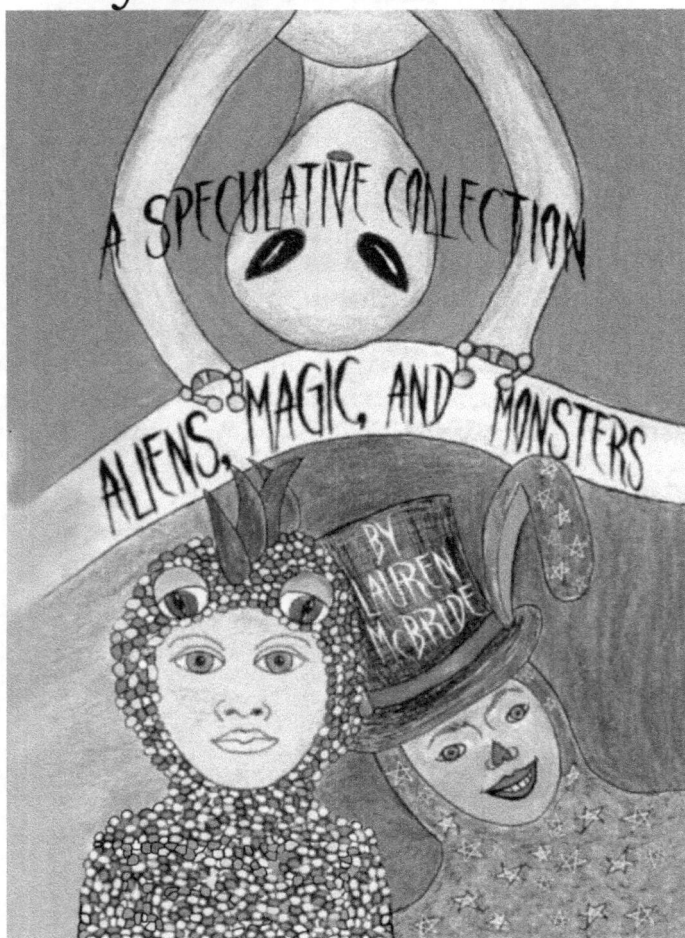

Fun to read. Fun to write. *Aliens, Magic, and Monsters* features poems set in the unlimited and imaginative realm of science fiction, fantasy, and horror. The poems were chosen to showcase over twenty poetic forms from acrostiku to zip, from strict rhyme to free verse, and much more in between. There are guidelines included on how to write each type of poem. Try a sci(na)ku. At only six words, it's sure to interest even the youngest readers.

Type: Juvenile and Young Adult Poetry Manual

Ordering links:
Print: https://www.hiraethsffh.com/product-page/aliens-magic-and-monsters-by-lauren-mcbride

ePub: https://www.hiraethsffh.com/product-page/aliens-magic-and-monsters-by-lauren-mcbride-2

PDF: https://www.hiraethsffh.com/product-page/aliens-magic-and-monsters-by-lauren-mcbride-1

The Stephen C. Curro Page

cultural appreciation
just for us
Martians recite Shakespeare

F-star glare
pushing aside
blue fronds

engine whine
flying through hyperspace
with the parking brake on

winter solstice
leaves made of fire
light the night

The Roxanne Barbour Page

Moon
dark side
gambling dens uncovered

dread of future
paralyzing humans
first contact

rain
dreadful occurrence
Martian dunes slump

fairy tales
concocted by Martians
involving Egyptian pyramids

The L.L. Hill Page

moth to light
a comet streaks
into the sun

solar spires spin
the ring of Phobos' remains
gleam in a blue dawn

blue sunrise
a rover bounces over
a Martian dune

The Randall Andrews Page

cutting emissions
witches switching over
electric broomsticks

mind readers marry
fidelity guaranteed
peace improbable

time travel trial
one week forward and back
lottery numbers

The Goran Lowie Page

at the end of time
we share a slow kiss
imagining the future

bleak wind
the dragon stirs
thin and brittle

near the wizard tower
I lose sight of my cat
wisps of fog

The Yuliia Vereta Page

the genuine me
just lost the final clone fight
no changes for lunch

good at transforming
I'm used to autotomy
still struggling with tail

they were mistaken
black holes are not teleports
I always had doubts

The Thomas Tilton Page

supernova
saying our final
goodbyes

particle accelerator
the beam
of your smile

in the escape pod
the closest
we've ever been

The Gary Davis Page

worn shutters rattle
ghosts can't make up their mind
stay or go

atom bomb blast
brings record show of hands
potter's field undead

thawing permafrost
zombie virus wakes up
real apocalypse

The Tyler McIntosh Page

scalp nodes
mainlining downloads
at the library

last in line
for the newest adapter
elbow rust

blood donation
I catch the nurse
licking her lips

The Herb Kauderer Page

robbed

our home universe
only existing timeline
without zeppelins

playing hookey

spaceship parking lot
a boy & his grandmother
gape at new models

traffic jam

dirigible cars
Venus's winds wreak havoc
late for work again

ETs Dancing
By Denise Noe

SCIFAIKU

three body problem
two suns above
how long will this summer last

Richard E Schell

red dust jitterbugging
in the shadow of Olympus Mons
Marsquake

Robert Borski

cataracted moon
winking at you
through telescope's eyepiece

Robert Borski

home planet
feeling the attraction
of long ago

Randy Brooks

joining my wife outside the lunar eclipse

Randy Brooks

science fiction pinup girl
everything weightless
but her breasts

Randy Brooks

the Icarus Project
embracing the madness
of the burning sun

Rick Jackofsky,

Designer human

humanoid enough
but the prehensile tail
can enhance coitus

Matthew Johnston

Parasite

the awkward moment
possession-transition-vertigo
switching meat suits

Matthew Johnston

teleporter broken walking to work

Greg Schwartz

The Gettysburg Address

all metal men created equally
united
against the human menace

    Matthew Wilson

Sleeping Beauty

sleeping for 1000 years
princess plugged into wall
only 5% charged

    Matthew Wilson

colony in mars
not enough oxygen
to fall in love

    Amitava Dasgupta

relationship
with alien woman
I become vegetarian

    Amitava Dasgupta

fifty years a
galaxy wanderer...
my own mapmaker

ayaz daryl nielsen

with more syllables
than we could possibly count
alien words for love

ayaz daryl nielsen

broadcast power
DDOS attack
aircar rain

David C. Kopaska-Merkel

2050
the year "Arctic ice"
became an oxymoron

T.R. Jones

tyrannosaur steaks
woolly mammoths on the grill
Time Traveler's Cafe

Stefan Thomas Boales

microscopic beasts
hitchhikers of the heavens
Andromeda's rain

Stefan Thomas Boales

watch a cyclone form
no precipitation here
why live on the moon

Ruben Horn

fuel cell froze again
I close the hood and gaze up
just like back out there

Ruben Horn

scrapyard
an orphan looks for the parts
to revive her brother

Ngo Binh Anh Khoa

nudist colony
all comfortable in their own skin,
scales, feathers, and fur

Ngo Binh Anh Khoa

new soccer size suns
heats home for a minimum
of two hundred years

Denny E. Marshall

beginning
of your third millennium
ennui kicks in

David C. Kopaska-Merkel

his time-machine car
took him back farther than planned
Jurassic parking

John H. Dromey

though nice in person
I prefer your avatar
let's meet in VR

John H. Dromey

cemetery...
    a whisper
        from below

Greg Schwartz

trophy hunter
the tiger paws through
what's left of him

Greg Schwartz

haunted cemetery
hanged by the neck
a bottle of ghosts

Guy Belleranti

her wisdom teeth

her wisdom teeth
take root in my mouth
should never have kissed her

Benjamin Whitney Norris

gulf war

drowned in the gulf
they climb the pier
no day at the beach

Benjamin Whitney Norris

lost kitten

lost kitten
found him
delicious

    Benjamin Whitney Norris

a man of mere bones
a suit of flesh
death disrobes him

    Brian Rosenberger

after the thunderstorms
eroded vegetable garden
his buried victims exposed

    Brian Rosenberger

highway accident
smart phone in your hand
half mile behind you

    Denny E. Marshall

with hand-eye coordination
the parasite delivered
insight

First Contact Haiga
By ARPY

MINIMAL POEM

the heart
extracted
still lives
beating
bursting
growing
organism perfected

Denise Noe

TANKA

shipwrecked
amid the tangled shadows
of Jupiter's moons
we divvy up the last packet
of freeze-dried ice cream

Rick Jackofsky,

Adrift

artificial gravity
and navigation busted
nothing here works
except the intercom
that plays only Debussy

Matthew Johnston

Gulp
the battle droid's head
spinning detached in the air
and time to wish
they didn't all
self-destruct

Matthew Johnston

express freight
the space manifolds
harbor arches of chaos
elegant shortcuts
inner to outer system
in merely a decade's time

Herb Kauderer

simulated sunset
over the solarium
she detassels me
I detassel her
in recycled mist

Randy Brooks

a parallel universe
where I was never born–
a chance to start over
with a new identity
and no bounty on my head

Ngo Binh Anh Khoa

OTHER FORMS
(including: Sijo, Fibonacci, Cinquain, Minutes, Diminuendo, Ghazals,Threesomes, Brick, etc.)

CHERITA

Gunfight At The Golden Zone Outpost

opportunities

we all will have them
challenged to the laser draw

crown the quickest in the zone
took it for granted
killer droids don't cry

Juan M. Perez

How To Lose When You're Winning

cry independence

we must always fight
where someone will have to lose

where winners will make the rules
except dirty nukes
then nothing matters

Juan M. Perez

GOGYOKA

pulchritude de morte
Herb Kauderer

a space criminal
floats outside the airlock
last breath after ejection
freezes in clusters
leaving a trail of red ice roses

SATURNE

best
villains
believe the
rightness of their
wrongs

Lauren McBride

FIBONACCI

at
last
he learns
his neighbor's
secret for growing
the largest beautiful flowers,
but he never tells
because he
is now
plant
food

Guy Belleranti

SCIFAIKU SESTET

A Scifaiku Sestet*
John J. Dunphy

"how would you like being called
'the fuck machine'?"
android prostitute replies
when her union rep asks
if she has any grievances

*What is a sestet? Read my article in the February 2022 issue of Scifaikuest.

JOINED POEMS

CHAINED SCI(NA)KU
Telling Time
timepieces
for starships -
typically three settings:

standard universal time,
homeworld and
local

Lauren McBride

First Contact

signal received
alien transmission
indecipherable

ten years later
intentions clarified
invasion fleet

T.R. Jones

Captain Clive's Log: Day 570

goldilocks zone
within a goldilocks zone
surely a paradise planet
of timid birds
and fat fruit for the taking.

Captain Clive's Log: Day 572

a planet too colorful
too much contrast
in sharp sun and shaded dark
the wind swaying trees whisper beauty
and scream danger.

Captain Clive's Journal: Day 573

dead crew
hearing their screams
as I drift in space
sparks red as blood on my hands
my log entries corrupted.

Matthew Johnston

NEW FROM HIRAETH PUBLISHING: Flash Digest, a quarterly publication of short fiction stories.

https://www.hiraethsffh.com/product-page/flash-digest-1

HAIBUN

"Shelter" by Greg Schwartz

Late afternoon. We stumble across an abandoned house. Some rotting planks in the shed and a rusty hammer. A few cans of beans. A lot of windows.

Only an hour of daylight left. It'll have to do.

> sliver of sunlight
> we board up
> the last window

ARTICLES

The Tutone Tanka by Stephen C. Curro

I have been experimenting with a new type of poetry. I don't know if anyone has ever done this, but it sounded like a fun idea to me. I was listening to the old song "867-5309/Jenny" by Tommy Tutone, and I decided to write a poem by writing each line in the same number of syllables for each number. If my math is right, there should be 38 syllables total. As there is a zero in the sequence, I decided to make that a space between the preceding lines and the final line. To justify why there is an odd space breaking the poem up, I decided to *make those final nine syllables something that drives the poem home,* kind of like the end of a sonnet.

So, here is the first success I had:

A trip to the Cretaceous is
almost worth it just for
that first breath of real air.
City air doesn't taste
half as good.

Then you see a rex, and you can't breathe...

I call it a Tutone Tanka. Here are more examples:

After years of painstaking work
I aim my telescope
to the stars. For the first time
we take real-time shots
of deep space...

Lightyears away, planets burn in war...

A Martian girl's first day on Earth,
teased because she can't run
in Earth's gravity or speak
with vocal chords like
"real people do."

She still offers hugs when someone cries.

There are days when I fly my ship
and the only flight plan
is full speed to empty space
before coming to
a dead stop...

...the only way to be truly still.

Controversial implants allow
a young musician to
invent the most intricate
guitar solos live
in concert...

...at the cost of short-term memory

*Based on the song title: "867-5309/Jenny" by Tommy Tutone,

By the Pound by Robert E. Porter

> *The apparition of these faces in the crowd:*
> *Petals on a wet, black bough.*
> --In a Station of the Metro, by Ezra Pound

"2013 is a year of celebration for English-language haiku," said the editors in their Forward. "It marks the centennial of the publication of the first fully realized haiku in English, Ezra Pound's 'In a Station of the Metro,' in P*oetry* magazine." (Kacian et al, xxii)

For their anthology, they collected haiku from a year before the Archduke Ferdinand's assassination to a dozen years after 9/11, including anti-war poems. In his Overview, editor Jim Kacian looked to the Imagists.

"They took to haiku, not surprisingly," he said, "since most of their stated goals directly overlapped with elements to be found in it: the aspiration to perceive the thing directly, to express it without emotion or excess, concisely and in common language. None was more a collector (and disperser) of influences than Ezra Pound." (Kacian,

311-312)

Pound -- that Pallas-like figure skulking and scheming behind *Ulysses* and teenage "Wasteland" Modernity.   Mu-wah-ha-ha-ha!

"Be influenced by as many great artists as you can," said Pound, "but have the decency either to acknowledge the debt outright, or to try to conceal it." (Pound, Imagiste)

Conceal your influences! Like a Ponzi, who conceals his debts in order to wheel-borrow more... That's a hellish descent compared to the decency of Michelangelo's David in a chic Che guerrilla outfit.

"The resuscitation of and collaboration with dead poets [Sextus Propertius, for ex.] is an important theme" in Pound's work, according to professor Alex Davis. (Davis, 23)

Propertius lived in the Roman world over 2000 years ago. He invented romance, at least in the context of a Tom Stoppard play. So, a proper subject to be hung in effigy and beaten like a piñata, or drowned in Poundian cantos, a slurry of obscure literary and historical references, contortionist phrasing and word salad, including Latin, Greek, and Chinese.

"That part of your poetry which strikes upon the imaginative eye of the reader," said Pound, "will lose nothing by translation into a foreign tongue; that which appeals to the ear can reach only those who take it in the original." (Pound, Imagiste)

I wonder: can *Finnegan's Wake* be successfully translated – into English, even? That extreme Joycean prosody appeals to the ear, maybe, like the sound poems of Kurt Schwitters, or a John Bonham drum solo. But the best haiku and scifaiku don't work that way; they strike the imaginative eye, tongue, nose, etc., translating words on a page into a sensation as easily understood as a boot to the head--

Or the sound of goosesteps marching to the Horst Wessel, the Internationale, or Giovinezza.

"Troublingly, though," said Davis, "the labour of these inter-war cantos contribute to an ongoing work of collaboration not only with source texts but also with Italian fascism." (Davis, 29)

In the context of WWII in Europe, "collaborators" sold out their neighbors and betrayed their nations to tyrants. Ezra Pound had a radio show in Italy while Mussolini's thugs (and later Nazis, during their occupation of the boot) stamped out dissent with threats, extortion, torture, and killings. Like that crypto-falangist prop *Ferdinand the Bull*, Pound preached against active resistance to bullies and butchers.

Why?

This line from a canto provides a clue:
And the dogmatic have to lie now and again
to maintain their conformity
(Pound, Cantos, 679)

In his novel *Mother Night*, Kurt Vonnegut explored the consequences of those lies, and that conformity. In his first-person narrative, poseur and playwright Howard W. Campbell, Jr. mimics Pound's dilemma:

"And the Republic's demands were framed so as to be educational, too – teaching that a propagandist of my sort was as much a murderer as Heydrich, Eichmann, Himmler, or any of the gruesome rest." (Vonnegut, 120)

Vonnegut named his character after John W. Campbell, Jr., a writer and editor as influential to science fiction as Pound was to literary Modernism. John's reputation later tanked with the promotion of L. Ron Hubbard's cult and his own contrarian arguments for segregation, the Vietnam War, etc. John was a ham radio operator, too; amateur, though. He never spoke for the Axis like Howard and Pound.

One of those two claimed to be a double agent. Of his handler, Howard said:

"He didn't mention the best reason for expecting me to go on and be a spy. The best reason was that I was a ham. As a spy of the sort he described, I would have an opportunity for some pretty grand acting. I would fool everyone with my brilliant interpretation of a Nazi, inside and out." (Vonnegut, 41)

Pound was more ham than operator. After the war, he might have stood trial for treason; insanity proved more convincing. He spent over a dozen years as a mental patient, mad about Confucius, relegated to literary crowd-surfing in New Directions and buzzing the hive-minds of pot-headed Beatniks. He died in November, after a Watergate summer, as the majority of Americans reelected Richard Nixon in 1972.

Towards the end of his own life, Vonnegut's Campbell said, "I was a political idiot, an artist who could not distinguish between reality and dreams." (Vonnegut, 189)

How like the man who birthed English-language haiku and Modernity! Who remains a crackpot, a conundrum, and a catalyst.

> *mother's day*
> *a nurse unties*
> *the restraints*
> (Roberta Beary, 206)

WORKS CITED

Beary, Roberta. "mother's day." *Haiku in English: The First Hundred Years*. W. W. Norton & Co., 2013.

Davis, Alex. "Collaborator: Ezra Pound, Translation, and Appropriation." *Modernist Cultures,* 14.1 (2019): p17–35.

Kacian, Jim. "An Overview of Haiku in English." *Haiku in English: The First Hundred Years.* W. W. Norton & Co., 2013.

Kacian, Jim and Philip Rowland and Allan Burns. "Editors' Forward." *Haiku in English: The First Hundred Years.* W. W. Norton & Co., 2013.

Pound, Ezra. "A Few Don'ts by an Imagiste." Poetry, March 2013. P200-206.

Pound, Ezra. *The Cantos of Ezra Pound.* New Directions, 1973.

Vonnegut, Kurt. *Mother Night.* Laurel, 1988.

NEW FROM HIRAETH PUBLISHING:

The Saint and the Robot by Gary Every

Albertus Magnus, an adolescent Thomas Aquinas, alchemy, three red-headed women, and a robot. What could go wrong?

https://www.hiraethsffh.com/product-page/saint and-the-robot-by-gary-every

FEATURED POET:
Lisa Timpf

SCIFAIKU

fusion chamber success—
making of heavier atoms
foreshadows a weight off Earth

Blue sunset on Mars—
so far away
the Earth, the Sun

morning walk—
beside her in the sim chamber
her childhood dog

goat yoga in space—
all fun and games
until gravity cuts out

ship escape's Earth's gravity—
seasoned space dog tramples air
curls up to nap

SENRYU

climate change is a myth
as the world burns
they warm their hands by the fire

JOINED SCIFAIKU

Climate Change Cha-Cha

adaptation—
sleep with the fish
underwater hotels

mitigation fails—
ice-melt floods coastal cities
hotels, underwater

DRAGONFLY FIBONACCI

Remember

space
bound,
passing
low orbit
the crew thinks of those
who traversed this space before them

Sputnik 2 roaring into orbit manned, not by man . . .

the crew prompted to think of dogs
known and loved, back home—
wet noses,
warm breath,
soft
ears

Laika's ghost restless today

FORTUNE COOKIE POEMS

You will make a change
for the better.

spaceport poker game—
in the pot
a ticket to Mars

Good things come
to those who wait.

giant spiderweb—
and he'd thought the fortune
was meant for him

You may accomplish more
by being direct.

first date—
he asks how she feels
about full-moon nights

Keep in touch
with your feelings.

mist-veiled bridge—
under the arch, a troll
scrawls poems

Now is a good time
for a bit of solitude

he cruises past Pluto Colony—
from here on, only the stars
for company

CHERITA

Exploring on Epsilon IV

booted feet raise dust

blocks of buildings
tower on either side

boxed in, we fear no ambush
wind's tuneless hum
the only sound

we seek life-signs

nothing, not even a microbe,
shows on our scans

who built these structures,
and why—the capricious breeze
chooses not to answer

what happened to you?

we long to shout
but whisper instead

clench of fear—
if we get an answer
will history repeat?

Getting Even

Grandchild shares favorite joke

Why was six afraid of seven?
Because! Seven "ate" nine!

Launchpad countdown
nine prepares
to seek revenge

Cherita

first contact specialist smiles

another language
discovered on Epsilon IV

he programs the 3D printer—
new letter tiles
for his favorite word game

ACROSTIKU

cat

curiosity brought it
across the light-years
terra is now home

DIDACTIC CINQUAIN

space
deadly vacuum
silent, massive, waiting
we hear its call
space

SIMON SIJO

Shielded

Red sand surrounds them
too toxic to support plants—
how, then, will they survive here?
The colonists craft a massive furnace,
a giant's glassworks, nuclear-powered.
Inside the craters
crops thrive in fields of compost,
shielded by glass forged from infertile sand.

Inspired by the book *Dinner on Mars*

HAIBUN

Off the Grid

News headline: Scientists have developed a 'living
PC' made from mushrooms

When fungi-driven computers hit the market in the
2030s, sales mushroomed. The mycelial web
quickly replaced the electronic one, and we learned
more about geology and the interconnectedness of
living things than we ever imagined. Understanding
our impact on other creatures changed our view of
what we really needed in order to be happy. We
rejected the consumption imperative drummed into
us by advertisers. Plummeting demand drove
factory closures.

> spanner in the works
> machinery of commerce
> grinds to a halt

People stopped working so hard. Those who could, left the cities to lead simpler lives. Others sought out green space within city limits, eschewing the walls that keep us from the world. We bartered instead of buying. Infrastructure crumbled, but by then, we'd reconciled ourselves to life off the grid. Some called it the end of civilization as we knew it. Others saw it as the start of the lives we were meant to live.

> spores of new possibility—
> so many ideas
> fruiting in our minds

Lisa Timpf's Bio:

Lisa Timpf's work experience has ranged from human resources and corporate communications to farm labor and stints as a sportswriter and a factory worker. A graduate of McMaster University's Physical Education program, Lisa also took several English and philosophy courses while attending university. Her work and life experiences, as well as her interest in nature, pets, and science, often find their way into her poetry.

Lisa's interest in writing speculative poetry and short stories began after her retirement in 2014. Since that time, she has had over 250 poems, the majority of them speculative, published. Her poetry has appeared in *Star*Line, Eye to the Telescope, New Myths, Scifaikuest, Polar Borealis*, and other venues. Lisa's collection of speculative haibun poetry, *In Days to Come*, is available from Hiraeth Publishing. When not writing, Lisa enjoys bird-watching and organic gardening. Check out lisatimpf.blogspot.com for information about Lisa's writing projects.

INTERVIEW WITH FEATURED POET Lisa Timpf

How long have you been writing poetry?
I've been writing poetry since grade school, though my first publication in a magazine came when I was in my early 20's.

Did you begin writing haiku before you branched out to scifaiku?
Yes. I wrote a fair bit of haiku, though only a few were published. Before trying scifaiku, I had some non-speculative haibun published in *Contemporary Haibun Online*.

How did you learn about scifaiku?
I first became aware of speculative poetry in general when I saw a submission call for Issue 16 of *Eye to the Telescope*, whose theme was "Music." Though the poem I submitted wasn't accepted for the issue, it later found a home elsewhere. Meanwhile, my interest in speculative poetry had been piqued. Not sure where—perhaps at the SFPA website—I heard about *Scifaikuest*, and decided to try writing scifaiku.

Where did you learn to write scifaiku?
The guidelines on the *Scifaikuest* site were my first introduction. I gradually refined my techniques by reading the Scifaiku written by others.

Do you write poetry other than genre poetry? If so, what kind?
I write some non-genre poetry, mainly about nature, pets, and personal experiences. Inspired by *Rattle's* "Poets Respond" feature, I also write poems, both genre and non-genre, based on news or magazine stories that catch my interest.

Whose poetry has influenced you the most?

While attending university, I took a number of English courses, so I would say the British poets I was exposed to had a degree of influence on my early writing—poets like Blake, Wordsworth, Donne, Eliot, and so on, as well as Canadian poet Robert W. Service. From the speculative front, I don't want to offend by leaving anyone out, but some of the poets whose work I have particularly admired include Marge Simon, F.J. Bergman, Amelia Gorman, LeRoy Gorman, Alan Ira Gordon, Sarah Tolmie, PS Cottier, Ada Hoffman, and LindaAnn Loschiavo, to name a few.

Who is your favorite poet?

It's tough to pick just one. I'd likely say Gerard Manley Hopkins—not necessarily all of his stuff, but there are particular poems that stand out for me, including "Spring and Fall, to a Young Child."

What/who is your main inspiration?

One of the underlying reasons for my interest in speculative poetry is *Star Trek: The Original Series*, along with novels by Andre Norton and Robert A. Heinlein. Exposure to these influences in my late teens and early twenties instilled a love for space opera, which in turn has influenced some of my imaginings about the future. I also draw inspiration for my poems from the things that interest me: nature, climate change, pets, science, family relationships, aging, and so on.

What poetry mags do you read/contribute to?

I generally read my contributor copies of *Star*Line* and *Scifaikuest*. In terms of contributing, I've been published in a variety of venues, including *New Myths, Polar Borealis, Polar Starlight, Eye to the Telescope, Space and Time,*

Thema, Spaceports & Spidersilk, Utopia Science Fiction, and *House of Zolo.*

FAVORITE POEM
by editor t.santitoro

mind readers marry
fidelity guaranteed
peace improbable

    Randall Andrews

Hahaha! I love this! So succinct! Well done!

Printed in the USA
CPSIA information can be obtained
at www.ICGtesting.com
CBHW020544270624
10675CB00027B/836